FUTURE DIRECTIONS FOR NSF ADVANCED COMPUTING INFRASTRUCTURE TO SUPPORT U.S. SCIENCE AND ENGINEERING IN 2017-2020

INTERIM REPORT

Committee on Future Directions for NSF Advanced Computing Infrastructure to Support U.S. Science in 2017-2020

Computer Science and Telecommunications Board

Division on Engineering and Physical Sciences

NATIONAL RESEARCH COUNCIL
OF THE NATIONAL ACADEMIES

THE NATIONAL ACADEMIES PRESS
Washington, D.C.
www.nap.edu

THE NATIONAL ACADEMIES PRESS   500 Fifth Street, NW   Washington, DC 20001

NOTICE: The project that is the subject of this report was approved by the Governing Board of the National Research Council, whose members are drawn from the councils of the National Academy of Sciences, the National Academy of Engineering, and the Institute of Medicine. The members of the committee responsible for the report were chosen for their special competences and with regard for appropriate balance.

This project was supported by the National Science Foundation, Award OCI-1344417. Any opinions, findings, or conclusions expressed in this publication are those of the author(s) and do not necessarily reflect the view of the organizations or agencies that provided support for this project.

International Standard Book Number-13:   978-0-309-31379-7
International Standard Book Number-10:   0-309-31379-1

Additional copies of this report are available from the National Academies Press, 500 Fifth Street, NW, Keck 360, Washington, DC 20001; (800) 624-6242 or (202) 334-3313; http://www.nap.edu.

Copyright 2014 by the National Academy of Sciences. All rights reserved.

Printed in the United States of America

THE NATIONAL ACADEMIES
Advisers to the Nation on Science, Engineering, and Medicine

The **National Academy of Sciences** is a private, nonprofit, self-perpetuating society of distinguished scholars engaged in scientific and engineering research, dedicated to the furtherance of science and technology and to their use for the general welfare. Upon the authority of the charter granted to it by the Congress in 1863, the Academy has a mandate that requires it to advise the federal government on scientific and technical matters. Dr. Ralph J. Cicerone is president of the National Academy of Sciences.

The **National Academy of Engineering** was established in 1964, under the charter of the National Academy of Sciences, as a parallel organization of outstanding engineers. It is autonomous in its administration and in the selection of its members, sharing with the National Academy of Sciences the responsibility for advising the federal government. The National Academy of Engineering also sponsors engineering programs aimed at meeting national needs, encourages education and research, and recognizes the superior achievements of engineers. Dr. C. D. Mote, Jr., is president of the National Academy of Engineering.

The **Institute of Medicine** was established in 1970 by the National Academy of Sciences to secure the services of eminent members of appropriate professions in the examination of policy matters pertaining to the health of the public. The Institute acts under the responsibility given to the National Academy of Sciences by its congressional charter to be an adviser to the federal government and, upon its own initiative, to identify issues of medical care, research, and education. Dr. Victor J. Dzau is president of the Institute of Medicine.

The **National Research Council** was organized by the National Academy of Sciences in 1916 to associate the broad community of science and technology with the Academy's purposes of furthering knowledge and advising the federal government. Functioning in accordance with general policies determined by the Academy, the Council has become the principal operating agency of both the National Academy of Sciences and the National Academy of Engineering in providing services to the government, the public, and the scientific and engineering communities. The Council is administered jointly by both Academies and the Institute of Medicine. Dr. Ralph J. Cicerone and Dr. C. D. Mote, Jr., are chair and vice chair, respectively, of the National Research Council.

www.national-academies.org

**COMMITTEE ON FUTURE DIRECTIONS FOR NSF
ADVANCED COMPUTING INFRASTRUCTURE
TO SUPPORT U.S. SCIENCE IN 2017-2020**

WILLIAM D. GROPP, University of Illinois, Urbana-Champaign, *Co-Chair*
ROBERT HARRISON, Stony Brook University, *Co-Chair*
MARK R. ABBOTT, Oregon State University
DAVID ARNETT, University of Arizona
ROBERT L. GROSSMAN, University of Chicago
PETER M. KOGGE, University of Notre Dame
PADMA RAGHAVAN, Pennsylvania State University
DANIEL A. REED, University of Iowa
VALERIE TAYLOR, Texas A&M University
KATHERINE A. YELICK, University of California, Berkeley

JON EISENBERG, Director, Computer Science and Telecommunications Board, and Study Director
SHENAE BRADLEY, Senior Program Assistant

COMPUTER SCIENCE AND TELECOMMUNICATIONS BOARD

ROBERT F. SPROULL, University of Massachusetts, Amherst, *Chair*
LUIZ ANDRÉ BARROSO, Google, Inc.
STEVEN M. BELLOVIN, Columbia University
ROBERT F. BRAMMER, Brammer Technology, LLC
EDWARD FRANK, Brilliant Lime and Cloud Parity
SEYMOUR E. GOODMAN, Georgia Institute of Technology
LAURA HAAS, IBM Corporation
MARK HOROWITZ, Stanford University
MICHAEL KEARNS, University of Pennsylvania
ROBERT KRAUT, Carnegie Mellon University
SUSAN LANDAU, Worcester Polytechnic Institute
PETER LEE, Microsoft Corporation
DAVID E. LIDDLE, US Venture Partners
BARBARA LISKOV, Massachusetts Institute of Technology
JOHN STANKOVIC, University of Virginia
JOHN A. SWAINSON, Dell, Inc.
ERNEST J. WILSON, University of Southern California
KATHERINE YELICK, University of California, Berkeley

Staff

JON EISENBERG, Director
VIRGINIA BACON TALATI, Program Officer
SHENAE BRADLEY, Senior Program Assistant
RENEE HAWKINS, Financial and Administrative Manager
HERBERT S. LIN, Chief Scientist
LYNETTE I. MILLETT, Associate Director
ERIC WHITAKER, Senior Program Assistant

For more information on CSTB, see its website at
http://www.cstb.org; write to CSTB, National Research Council,
500 Fifth Street, NW, Washington, DC 20001; call (202) 334-2605; or
e-mail CSTB at cstb@nas.edu.

Preface

Advanced computing, a term used in this report to include both compute- and data-intensive capabilities, is used to tackle a rapidly growing range of challenging science and engineering problems. The National Science Foundation (NSF) requested that the National Research Council (NRC) carry out a study examining anticipated priorities and associated trade-offs for advanced computing in support of NSF-sponsored science and engineering research. The study encompasses advanced computing activities and programs throughout NSF, including but not limited to, those of its Division on Advanced Cyberinfrastructure. The statement of task for the full NRC study is given in Box P.1. In response to this request, the NRC established the Committee on Future Directions for NSF Advanced Computing Infrastructure to Support U.S. Science in 2017-2020 (see Appendix A). As part of the study, the sponsor also requested an interim report in 2014 that identifies key issues and discusses potential options.

The committee has begun its work by gathering and reviewing relevant materials, receiving testimony and comments from individuals, and identifying additional experts to receive testimony from and additional sources of information. The information collection is still incomplete, but some important issues have begun to come into focus. Mindful that NSF seeks timely input for its budget process and that the issues raised in the study merit broad input from the science and engineering communities that use, develop, and provide advanced computing capabilities, the study committee offers this interim report to frame issues it believes that

> **BOX P.1**
> **Statement of Task**
>
> A study committee will examine anticipated priorities and associated trade-offs for advanced computing in support of National Science Foundation (NSF)-sponsored science and engineering research. Advanced computing capabilities are used to tackle a rapidly growing range of challenging science and engineering problems, many of which are compute-, communications-, and data-intensive as well. The committee will consider:
>
> 1. The contribution of high-end computing to U.S. leadership and competitiveness in basic science and engineering and the role that NSF should play in sustaining this leadership;
> 2. Expected future national-scale computing needs: high-end requirements, those arising from the full range of basic science and engineering research supported by NSF, as well as the computing infrastructure needed to support advances in modeling and simulation as well as data analysis;
> 3. Complementarities and trade-offs that arise among investments in supporting advanced computing ecosystems; software, data, communications;
> 4. The range of operational models for delivering computational infrastructure, for basic science and engineering research, and the role of NSF support in these various models; and
> 5. Expected technical challenges to affordably delivering the capabilities needed for world-leading scientific and engineering research.
>
> An interim report will identify key issues and discuss potential options. It might contain preliminary findings and early recommendations. A final report will include a framework for future decision making about NSF's advanced computing strategy and programs. The framework will address such issues as how to prioritize needs and investments and how to balance competing demands for cyberinfrastructure investments. The report will emphasize identifying issues, explicating options, and articulating trade-offs and general recommendations.
>
> The study will not make recommendations concerning the level of federal funding for computing infrastructure.

NSF and the committee itself need to consider, and to stimulate discussion and encourage feedback to the committee on these issues.

What follows is an initial compilation of issues that the committee believes will need to be considered as future NSF strategy, budgets, and programs for advanced computing are developed, together with key issues on which the committee invites comment. This list is preliminary, and the committee anticipates adding to and refining this list as it prepares its final report. Appendix B provides a supplemental set of questions focused on the needs of users of advanced computing on which the committee also invites comment.

Some issues will require further input and deliberation before the committee comments on them. For example, the committee has not yet devoted much attention to Item 1 in the statement of task, regarding the contribution of high-end computing to U.S. leadership and competiveness and the role that NSF should play in sustaining this leadership. It has also not addressed issues around data curation, access, and sustainability, which, although not central to the committee's task, will nonetheless be important elements of NSF's future strategy for advanced computing.

We invite your feedback on this report and, more generally, your comments on the future of advanced computing at NSF. You may provide feedback by email to <sciencecomputing@nas.edu> or via the project's public feedback page at <www.nas.edu/sciencecomputing>.

William D. Gropp and Robert Harrison, *Co-Chairs*
Committee on Future Directions for NSF
Advanced Computing Infrastructure to
Support U.S. Science in 2017-2020

Acknowledgment of Reviewers

This report has been reviewed in draft form by individuals chosen for their diverse perspectives and technical expertise, in accordance with procedures approved by the National Research Council's Report Review Committee. The purpose of this independent review is to provide candid and critical comments that will assist the institution in making its published report as sound as possible and to ensure that the report meets institutional standards for objectivity, evidence, and responsiveness to the study charge. The review comments and draft manuscript remain confidential to protect the integrity of the deliberative process. We wish to thank the following individuals for their review of this report:

Amy W. Apon, Clemson University,
Daniel E. Atkins III, University of Michigan,
Thom H. Dunning, Northwest Institute for Advanced Computing,
Susan L. Graham, University of California, Berkeley,
Laura Haas, IBM Research,
Tony Hey, Microsoft Research,
Michael L. Klein, Temple University, and
Linda Petzold, University of California, Santa Barbara.

Although the reviewers listed above have provided many constructive comments and suggestions, they were not asked to endorse the conclusions or recommendations, nor did they see the final draft of the report before its release. The review of this report was overseen by Elsa M. Garmire,

Dartmouth College. Appointed by the National Research Council, she was responsible for making certain that an independent examination of this report was carried out in accordance with institutional procedures and that all review comments were carefully considered. Responsibility for the final content of this report rests entirely with the authoring committee and the institution.

Contents

SUMMARY 1

1 THE ROLE OF ADVANCED COMPUTING IN SCIENCE AND ENGINEERING 7
  Complementary Roles of Simulation and Data-Intensive Computing, 9

2 CHALLENGES 11
  Responding to Growing Demand, 11
    Growing Demand, 11
    The Potential of Data-Intensive Computing for NSF Science and Engineering and the Corresponding Requirements, 11
    Workflow, 12
  Technology Challenges, 12
    Compute-Intensive Challenges, 12
    Data-Intensive Challenges, 13
    Serving Both Data- and Compute-Intensive Workloads, 14
    Software and Algorithms for Next Generation Cyberinfrastructure, 15
    Training the Next Generation of Scientists, 15
  Demand and Resource Allocation, 16
    Demand for Capacity, 16
    Demand for Capability, 16

The Role of the Private Sector in Providing Advanced
    Computing, 17
The Role of Other Federal Agencies in Providing Advanced
    Computing, 17
Allocation of Research Funding and Computing
    Resources, 18

3   POSSIBLE NSF RESPONSES   19
    Better Understanding of Science and Engineering
        Opportunities, Priorities, and Requirements for
        Advanced Computing, 19
    Functional Rather than Technology-Focused or Structural
        Approach to Understanding Requirements and
        Establishing Priorities, 20
    Enhanced Organizational Stability and Flexibility of
        NSF-Funded Advanced Computing Centers, 21
    Enhanced Strategic Planning and Internal Coordination, 21

APPENDIXES

A   Biographies of Committee Members   25
B   Questions on Directions and Needs for Advanced   32
        Cyberinfrastructure

Summary

The National Science Foundation (NSF) asked the National Research Council to study anticipated priorities and associated trade-offs for advanced computing in support of NSF-sponsored science and engineering research. (See Box P.1 in the Preface for the complete statement of task.) This interim report contains a preliminary set of issues the Committee on Future Directions for NSF Advanced Computing Infrastructure to Support U.S. Science in 2017-2020 believes that NSF, the science and engineering research community, and the committee itself need to consider. It is intended to stimulate discussion and prompt feedback that the committee will consider in preparing its final report. (See the Preface for how to provide feedback to the study committee.)

BUILDING ADVANCED COMPUTING INFRASTRUCTURE TO SUPPORT INTEGRATED DISCOVERY

Advanced computing in this context refers to the technical capabilities that support compute- and data-intensive research across the entire science and engineering spectrum and that are so expensive that they are shared among multiple researchers, institutions, and applications. Compute-intensive modeling and simulation, the historical focus of high-performance computing systems and programs, is an established peer, standing beside theory and experimentation, in the scientific process. Data-intensive computing is emerging as a "fourth paradigm" for scientific discovery, complementing theory, experiment, and simulation, and may require new technical and programmatic responses. Compute- and data-intensive approaches are increasingly used in combination: data is used to validate models, simulations are used to quantify uncertainty or fill in for incomplete theory, and stochastic models link modeling and data analytics. Data-intensive computing is becoming more important as the volume of data grows, as new analytical techniques are adopted, and as some fields move from being primarily compute-intensive to being much more data-intensive.

For its final report, the committee will explore and seeks comment on

    1. How to create advanced computing infrastructure that enables integrated discovery involving experiments, observations, analysis, theory, and simulation.

TECHNOLOGY CHALLENGES

Unfavorable trends in power consumption and inter-chip communications are forcing consideration of new system architectures, the development of new algorithms and software approaches to use them, and more attention to redundancy and fault tolerance. Absent new technology, the anticipated end of sustained reductions in the ratio of price to performance (a benefit of Moore's Law) portends stagnation in computer performance improvement. For data-intensive systems, variability in storage hardware performance and failure rates constrain the performance and practical size of very-large-scale systems. Also, it will not be straightforward in all cases to keep scaling up system and scientific software to meet growing needs. The resulting uncertainty about technical direction complicates planning for future extreme-performance computers.

Today's approach of federating distributed compute- and data-intensive resources to meet the increasing demand for combined computing and data capabilities is technically challenging and expensive. New approaches that co-locate computational and data resources might reduce costs and improve performance. Recent advances in cloud data center design may provide a viable integrated solution for a significant fraction of (but not all) data- and compute-intensive and combined workloads.

New algorithms and software approaches will be needed to effectively use systems with new architectures, and they can also play an important role in continuing to improve the performance of scientific codes and the productivity of researchers. Some developments may best take place within individual research areas and disciplines, but others may benefit from common, coordinated efforts.

SUMMARY   3

New knowledge and skills will be needed to effectively use these new advanced computing technologies. "Hybrid" disciplines such as computational science and data science and interdisciplinary teams may come to play an increasingly important role.

For its final report, the committee will explore and seeks comments on

2. Technical challenges to building future, more capable advanced computing systems and how NSF might best respond to them.

RESPONDING TO GROWING DEMAND

Demand for advanced computing has been growing for all types and capabilities of systems, from large numbers of single-commodity nodes to jobs requiring thousands of cores; for systems with fast interconnects; for systems with excellent data handling and management; and for an increasingly diverse set of applications that includes data analytics as well as modeling and simulation.

Anecdotal reports point to a low and perhaps declining rate of success for obtaining allocation of time on existing machines. Given the "double jeopardy" that arises when researchers must clear two hurdles—first, to obtain funding for their research proposal and, second, to be allocated the necessary computing resources—the chances that a researcher with a good idea can carry out the proposed work under such conditions is diminished.

Since the advent of its supercomputing centers, NSF has provided its researchers with state-of-the-art computing systems. But it is unclear, given their likely cost, whether NSF will be able to invest in future highest-tier systems in the same class as those being pursued by the Department of Energy, Department of Defense, and other federal mission agencies and overseas. Options for providing highest-tier capabilities that merit further exploration include purchasing computing services from federal agencies (thus increasing access beyond that driven by direct mission interests) or by making arrangements with commercial services (rather than more expensive purchases by individual researchers).

More broadly, across a wide spectrum of system capability, the growth of new models of computing, including cloud computing and publically available but privately held data repositories, opens up new possibilities for NSF. Access to these commercial facilities could widen access to large-scale capabilities for computation and data analytics, but the cost trade-offs are complicated and need to be looked at carefully.

It is becoming increasingly difficult to balance investments in advanced computing facilities, given the large and growing aggregate demand, the steep cost of the highest-end systems, growing demand for data-intensive as well as compute-intensive systems, and the constant or shrinking NSF resources. Compounding the challenge is the wide variety of computing needs, the state of scientific data and software, and wide variation in ability to effectively use advanced computing across scientific disciplines. Moreover, the range of science and engineering research sponsored by NSF involves a diverse set of workflows, including those that involve primarily compute- or data-intensive processing and ones that involve combinations of both.

It is thus harder than ever to understand the expanding and diverse requirements of the science and engineering community; explain the importance of a new, broader range of advanced computing infrastructure to stakeholders, including those that set budgets; explore non-traditional approaches; and manage the advanced computing portfolio strategically.

3. The committee will review data from NSF and the advanced computing programs it supports and seeks input, especially quantitative data, on the computing needs of individual research areas.

For its final report, the committee seeks comment on

4. The match between resources and demand for the full spectrum of systems, for both compute- and data-intensive applications, and the impacts on the research community if NSF can no longer provide state-of-the-art computing for its research community.

5. The role that private industry and other federal agencies can play in providing advanced computing infrastructure—including the opportunities, costs, issues, and service models, as well as balancing the different costs and making trade-offs in accessibly (e.g., guaranteeing on-demand access is more costly than providing best-effort access).

6. The challenges facing researchers in obtaining allocations of computing resources and suggestions for improving the allocation and review processes for making advanced computing resources available to the research community.

POSSIBLE NSF RESPONSES

Better Understanding of Science and Engineering Opportunities, Priorities, and Requirements for Advanced Computing

Not all research areas or programs have defined their requirements for advanced computing or established processes for regularly updating and refining them, such as by constructing roadmaps that describe science or engineering goals and advanced computing resources needed.

Such analyses may provide useful information for understanding aggregate capability and capacity needs and expected trends in these needs, for understanding overall NSF resource requirements, for prioritizing investments, and for better aligning research programs and supporting advanced computing investments. Because scientists can effectively use infrastructure only when it is presented as an integrated whole—encompassing appropriate hardware, software, data, networking, technical services, and so forth; it may be most productive to use a functional rather than a technology-focused or structural approach focused on individual elements.

For its final report, the committee will explore and seeks comment on

7. *Whether wider collection and more frequent updating of requirements for advanced computing could be used to inform strategic planning, priority setting, and resource allocation; how these requirements might be used; and how they might best be developed, collected, aggregated, and analyzed.*

Enhanced Organizational Stability and Flexibility of NSF-Funded Advanced Computing Centers

Although NSF's use of frequent open competitions has stimulated intellectual competition and increased NSF's financial leverage, it has also impeded collaboration among frequent competitors, made it more difficult to recruit and retain talented staff, and inhibited longer-term planning.

For its final report, the committee seeks comment on

8. *The tension between the benefits of competition and the need for continuity as well as alternative models that might more clearly delineate the distinction between performance review and accountability and organizational continuity and service capabilities.*

Enhanced Strategic Planning and Internal Coordination

Advanced computing receives less attention in the current NSF strategic plan than might be expected, given its vital role in science and engineering, although it is the subject of a separate strategy focused on cyberinfrastructure. Decision making about advanced computing is distributed across the Division for Advanced Cyberinfrastructure, other divisions and division programs, the Major Research Instrumentation Program, and individual research institutions. Both coordination and strategic decision making seem especially important in an era of growing demand and cost. Top-down mandates often prove ineffective, even when the coordination is very much needed, and reaching consensus through "grass-roots" efforts may be too slow. Both top-down and bottom-up processes require mechanisms for identifying detailed needs of the directorates and their programs and for ensuring adequate community input.

For its final report, the committee seeks comment on

9. How NSF might best coordinate and set overall strategy for advanced computing-related activities and investments as well as the relative merits of both formal, top-down coordination and enhanced, bottom-up process.

1

The Role of Advanced Computing in Science and Engineering

Many past reports have underscored the integral role of advanced computing in science and engineering, including but not limited to the role of computing in addressing scientific and engineering "grand challenges" vital to our nation's welfare, security, and competitiveness. Over time, and especially in recent years, advanced computing has become relevant to an expanding set of scientific problems and disciplines.

The term *advanced computing* is used in this report to refer to the full complement of capabilities that support compute- and data-intensive research across the entire science and engineering spectrum, which are too expensive to be purchased by an individual research group or department and perhaps too expensive even for an individual research institution. The term also encompasses higher-end computing for which there are economies of scale in establishing shared facilities rather than having each institution acquire, maintain, and support its own systems. For compute-intensive research, it includes not only today's "supercomputers," which are able to perform more than 10^{15} floating point operations per second (known as "petascale") but also "high-performance computing" platforms that share the same technologies as supercomputers but may have lower levels of performance.

The terms capability and capacity are sometimes used to refer to the low and high end of the spectrum of computing performance of a single application. *Capability computing* is computing that stretches the limits of available resources. For example, for compute-intensive applications, it is the capability to run the largest possible tightly coupled computations (i.e., which can only be run practically on a single computer system). The concept of capability computing also applies to data-intensive applications, although how this might best be defined is an open question. Faster machines have been deployed by the Department of Energy and elsewhere; these very fastest machines might be thought of as the "extreme end."

Capacity computing, by contrast, provides large amounts of computing but lower peak performance. What was capability computing 2 decades ago is capacity computing today, both in terms of individual computing needs and the number of jobs being run. The distinction is arguably somewhat artificial: high-performance computers cover a wide range of performance characteristics, and large machines can be used to provide either capacity or capability. The need for researchers to reach solutions in a reasonable amount of time means that any large problem or large ensemble of problems, even those that do not require a capability machine to reach a solution, can be in some sense a capability problem. *High-throughput computing* refers to systems that provide large amounts of processing capacity over long periods of time—that is, the number of operations available per month or year rather than per second—but not as high peak performance.

Since the beginning of the National Science Foundation's (NSF's) supercomputing centers program in the 1980s, NSF's Division of Advanced Cyberinfrastructure (ACI) and its predecessor organizations have supported computational research across NSF with both supercomputers and other high-performance computers and provided services to a user base that spans work sponsored by all federal research agencies.

Modeling and simulation has for some time been seen as a true peer, standing beside theory and experiment, in the scientific process. It is used at a wide range of scales, as measured by the number of parallel cores needed. Some problems in astrophysics, cosmology, or biomolecular modeling use massively parallel simulations and run on machines with tens to hundreds of thousands (or more) cores. Other problems, in fields such as materials, climate simulation, and earthquake modeling, use large volumes of computation on "midscale" machines with a thousand or more cores, as do a wide array of applications of uncertainty quantification and other techniques for robust design and decision making. In addition, massive volumes of high-throughput simulations are used in combinatorial chemistry, drug design, design of functional materials, and systems design.

Data-intensive computing is beginning to emerge as a separate discipline and is being viewed by some as a "fourth paradigm" for scientific discovery, complementing discoveries made by theory, experiment, and simulation. In some disciplines, such as astronomy and biology, the percentage of research papers that are primarily based on data from data repositories of previously collected data, versus new experimental data, is increasing and reaching a point that this mode of discovery is now a significant driver of research. Networked sensors are increasingly embedded in urban and civil infrastructure, and sensors are widely used to capture research data in a growing number of fields. New algorithms for analyzing data sets that are large, complex, noisy, or unstructured allow automatic discovery of patterns within data that were previously unknown. Web search engines, online shopping recommendations, and face recognition software are some well-known applications of such algorithms, but these techniques are also increasingly valuable in science and engineering. Internet companies, such as Google, Yahoo!, Facebook, and Amazon, have introduced new software and hardware platforms and new programming models for data-intensive computing, and these platforms and models are increasingly being used for scientific research. Data-intensive research may require high-performance input/output (I/O) systems, access to very large storage systems using systems with different architectures than traditional high-performance computing systems, and new approaches to data visualization.

COMPLEMENTARY ROLES OF SIMULATION AND DATA-INTENSIVE COMPUTING

NSF's historical emphasis on advanced computing for modeling and simulation is sometimes viewed as being in competition with the more recent interest in data-intensive computing. The relative need for one or the other is important when future advanced computing investments are considered, because the types of computer systems, storage systems, networks, software, usage models, staffing and support, industry partners, and organizational structures may be different (and possibly quite different) across these two broad categories of use. The needs of users in the two categories and the appropriate technical and organizational responses to those needs both require future study.

It is misleading, however, to think of these two categories as competing in science and engineering, because modeling and data analysis are often used in concert. In cosmology, computational models are used to fill in missing or incomplete data; in image-based scientific instruments such as synchrotrons, simulation may be used to "invert" the observation into a particular crystal structure; in climate analysis, reconstruction of historical data is critical to the validation of models; and in the Materials Genome Initiative, the results of millions of simulations are being stored and shared for community analysis. Large experiments in fields like high-energy physics use simulation to design devices and to set up individual experiments to maximize the likelihood of success. Simulations produce large data sets that are part of the data challenge, and sophisticated simulations incorporate observational data to quantify uncertainty or fill in for incomplete theory. Advanced computational models and algorithms are being fused with observational data and with more sophisticated and expensive techniques to accommodate and quantify uncertainty. Fundamentally, scientific discovery goes beyond identifying patterns in data to discovering models that explain and predict those patterns. As these examples suggest, the fusion of computational modeling and data analytics pervades all of science and engineering. This is true of both large scientific collaborations and the work of individual investigators.

Modeling and large-scale data analysis is also driving the development of a new class of stochastic models in many areas of research, such as Earth system modeling. The present class of dynamically based models are being stretched to their limits because there is often little knowledge of the model parameters, let alone the dynamical form of critical processes such as cloud formation and rainfall. Rather than continuing to improve model resolution and add more features, some climate researchers are advocating for a new approach based on stochastic models that will link models and large-scale data analytics.

Thus, for many scientific disciplines, the issue is not whether to use data or simulation, but how the two will be used together. The need for advanced computing is important throughout disciplines, as the models, data, and types of scientific inquiry grow in sophistication. The increasing number of uses that combine computational models and observational data suggests that facilities supporting both are needed, and there may be value in co-locating data and compute capabilities. Although the technical challenges are many, the social, organizational, and funding challenges may be equally crucial.

1. For its final report, the committee will explore and seeks comments on how to create advanced computing infrastructure that enables integrated discovery involving experiments, observations, analysis, theory, and simulation.

2

Challenges

RESPONDING TO GROWING DEMAND

Growing Demand

Demand for capacity and capability computing has been growing both in terms of computing requirements and the number of scientists and researchers involved. It is becoming increasingly difficult to balance investments, given the large and growing aggregate demand, the high cost of high-end facilities, and the constant or shrinking National Science Foundation (NSF) resources. Compounding the challenge is the wide variety across scientific disciplines in terms of computing needs, the state of scientific data and software, and the ability of researchers to effectively use advanced computing.

These developments present new challenges for NSF as it seeks to understand the expanding requirements of the science and engineering community; explain the importance of a new broader range of advanced computing infrastructure to stakeholders, including those that set its budget; explore non-traditional approaches; and manage the advanced computing portfolio strategically.

The Potential of Data-Intensive Computing for NSF Science and Engineering and the Corresponding Requirements

Multiple fields (e.g., materials science) are also transitioning from being primarily compute-intensive (e.g., ab initio simulations in material science) to being much more data-intensive (e.g., due to the rapid growth of experimental data, growing use of data analytics, and automation of calculations searching for materials with desired properties) and may not be prepared for this transition. Some communities may lack sufficient national or communal hardware or software infrastructure to facilitate development of new workflows or to realize economies of scale and may not have leveraged best practices and investments established by other communities.

Workflow

Workflow refers to the series of computational steps required to yield a research result from the experimental and/or simulation results and to the tools and processes used to manage them and record the provenance of results. The range of science and engineering research sponsored by NSF involves a diverse set of workflows, including those that involve primarily compute- or data-intensive processing or combinations of both. Additionally, the compute and data capacities and the scale of parallelism required by these workflows can vary greatly by several orders of magnitude. The shift from general-purpose central processing units (CPUs) to more specialized architectures, such as hybrids of general-purpose processors and graphical processing units, which have a much more highly parallel structure, further exacerbates the challenges of aligning the workflows with available computing capabilities.

TECHNOLOGY CHALLENGES

A number of technology challenges will affect the ability of NSF and others to deliver the desired advanced computing capabilities to the science and engineering communities. They will require adaptations, such as recoding existing software and writing new software in new ways, while providing new opportunities for advanced computing users to make the necessary adaptations.

Compute-Intensive Challenges

It is an accepted truth today that Moore's Law will end sometime in the next decade, causing significant impact to high-end systems. We have already transitioned through a major technology-driven change in 2004, driven by hitting a "power wall" in our ability to cool processor chips, which has already rewritten the architectural landscape. Already, graphics processing units (GPUs) are providing a significant increase in computing power per chip and per unit energy, but often at the cost of needing new algorithms and new software. Data exchange capabilities between processors are also under increasing pressure, because as the number of transistors and cores on a die continues to explode, the number of paths and rate at which we can signal over such paths is growing, at best, slowly. These trends are forcing consideration of new architectures—possibly distinct from the ones used to build conventional mid-range systems—and new software approaches in order to use them effectively. Indeed, future growth in capabilities may come from an explosion of specialized hardware architectures that exploit the growth in the number of transistors on a chip. The transition implied by the anticipated end of Moore's Law will be even more severe—absent development of disruptive technologies; it could mean, for the first time in over three decades, the stagnation of computer performance and the end of sustained reductions in the price-performance ratio. Redundancy and fault tolerant algorithms are also likely to become more important. Lastly, power consumption (and its associated costs) is now a significant factor in the design of any large data center. For example, simple extrapolation of existing climate models to resolve processes such as cloud formation quickly lead to a computer that requires costly and possibly impractical amounts of electrical power. These challenges and the associated uncertainty pose significant challenges when contemplating future investment in extreme performance computers.

Data-Intensive Challenges

Building data-intensive systems that provide the needed scale and performance will require attention to several technical challenges. These include the following:

• *Managing variability and failure in storage components.* Very-large-scale, data-intensive computing consists of large numbers of storage devices (typically disks), which are often commodity components and not the higher-quality storage devices generally used in high-performance computing. Although the probability of failure of any single device is low, the aggregate number of failures is high, as is the variability in time required for a device to perform a computation (those that take longer than would be expected from the performance of their peers are sometimes called stragglers). For example, a large part of the complexity of systems like Hadoop is the result of dealing with failures and stragglers. Research is needed to more efficiently manage failure and variance, especially for a broader range of programming models.

• *Very-large-scale scientific data management and analysis.* Although this is an active research area, it is still a challenge to manage data at the petabyte (PB) to exabyte scale. File systems, data management systems, data querying systems, provenance systems, data analysis systems, statistical modeling systems, workflow systems, visualization systems, collaboration systems, and data sharing must all scale together. Data analysis is typically an iterative process, and traditional scientific computing approaches often rely on software that was never designed to work at this scale. As a simple example, there is no open-source file or storage system that scales to 100 PB. On the other hand, the commercial sector has developed data management infrastructure over distributed file systems, which has produced a variety of new data management systems, sometimes called NoSQL (not only SQL) systems. We are moving into an era of data access through a set of application programming interfaces (APIs) rather than discrete files. Adapting scientific software will be a challenge in this new environment.

• *At scale interoperability of geographically distributed data centers.* Very-large–scale, data-intensive computing relies more on external data resources than is usually the case with high-performance computing. Some of the most interesting discoveries in data science have been made by integrating third-party and external data. Analysis that uses data distributed across multiple locations requires costly, high-capacity network links, and its performance will in any event suffer compared to computation that uses data in a single location. For this reason, data-center-scale computing platforms benefit by integrating at scale with other such facilities and the data repositories they contain.

Serving Both Data- and Compute-Intensive Workloads

As discussed above, research increasingly involves both compute- and data-intensive computing. What technical and system architectural approaches are best suited to handling this mix is an open question. Federating distributed compute- and data-intensive resources has repeatedly been found to present multiple additional costs and challenges, including, but not limited to, network latency and bandwidth, resource scheduling, security, and software licensing and versioning. Overcoming these challenges could increase participation and diversify resources and might be essential to realizing new science and engineering frontiers by coupling capability computing with experiments producing large data. Avoiding unnecessary federation by consciously co-locating facilities might yield significant cost savings and enhancements to both performance and capability. An additional complication is that many important scientific data collections are not currently hosted in existing scientific computing centers.

Recent advances in cloud data center design (including commodity processors and networks and virtualization of these resources) may make it cost-effective for data centers to serve a significant fraction of both data-intensive and compute-intensive workloads. Such an approach might also support different use models, such as access via cloud APIs, that complement traditional batch queues. This may prove essential to opening NSF resources to use by new communities and enabling greater utilization. Co-location of computing and data will be an important aspect of these new environments, and such approaches may work best when the bulk of the data exchange can be kept inside a data center.

Software and Algorithms for Next Generation Cyberinfrastructure

As described above, most experts believe that the coming end of Moore's Law and the long domination of complementary metal-oxide-semiconductor (CMOS) devices in computing will force significant changes in computer architecture. Successful exploitation of these new architectures will require the development of new software and algorithms that can use them effectively. New software and algorithms will also be needed for computation that uses cloud computing architectures.

New algorithms and software techniques can also help improve the performance of codes and the productivity of researchers. Adoption of either will depend on establishing incentives for their adoption into existing applications and use of appropriate metrics to evaluate the effectiveness of applications in context. For example, a code that only needs to run for, at most, a few hundred hours may not need to be very efficient, but one that will run for a million hours should be demonstrably efficient in terms of total run time, not floating-point operations per second (FLOPS).

Relaxing the "near-perfect" accuracy of computing may usher in a new era of "approximate computing" to address system failures, including data corruption, given the massive scale of these new systems. Any investment in cyberinfrastructure will need to take into account the need to update, and in many cases redevelop, the software infrastructure for research that has been developed over the past few decades. Under these conditions, innovations in algorithms, numerical methods, and theoretical models may play a much greater role in future advances in computational capability.

Training the Next Generation of Scientists

New knowledge and skills will be needed to make effective use of new system architectures and software. "Hybrid" disciplines such as computational science and data science and interdisciplinary teams may come to play an increasingly important role. Keeping abreast of a rapidly evolving suite of relevant technologies is challenging for many computer science programs, especially those with limited partnerships with the private sector. Most domain scientists rely on traditional software tools and languages and may not have ready access to knowledge or expertise about new approaches.

2. The committee will explore and seeks comments on the technical challenges to building future, more capable advanced computing systems and how NSF might best respond to them.

DEMAND AND RESOURCE ALLOCATION

Demand for Capacity

Comments from the science and engineering communities anecdotally suggest a pent-up demand for advanced computing resources, such as unsatisfied Extreme Science and Engineering Discovery Environment (XSEDE) allocation requests for already peer-reviewed and NSF-funded research. This need is across all types and capabilities of systems, from large numbers of single-commodity-nodes to jobs requiring thousands of cores, fast interconnects, and excellent data handling and management.

Demand for Capability

Since the beginnings of the NSF supercomputing centers, NSF has provided its researchers with state-of-the-art capability computing systems. Today, the Blue Waters system at Illinois and Stampede at Texas represent significant infrastructure for capability computing, augmented by other systems that are part of XSEDE. Today, it is unclear whether NSF will be able to invest in future highest-tier capability systems. Mission-oriented agencies in the United States, such as the Department of Energy, as well as international research organizations, such as the Partnership for Advanced Computing in Europe or the Ministry of Science and Technology in China, are pursuing systems that are at least an order of magnitude more powerful, for both computation and data handling, than current NSF systems. Similarly, commercial cloud systems, while not an alternative for the kinds of applications that require tightly coupled capability systems, have massive aggregate computing and data-handling power.

3. The committee will review data from NSF and the advanced computing programs it supports and seeks input, especially quantitative data, on the computing needs of individual research areas.

4. The committee seeks comments on the match between resources and demand for the full spectrum of systems, for both compute- and data-intensive applications, and the impacts on the research community if NSF can no longer provide state-of-the-art computing for its research community.

The Role of the Private Sector in Providing Advanced Computing

Historically, NSF has supported the acquisition of specialized research infrastructure through a variety of processes, including Major Research Equipment and Facilities Construction and Major Research Instrumentation programs, support for major centers, and individual grants. In many cases, the private sector has provided equipment and expertise, but the private sector has not provided NSF researchers with a significant source of computing cycles or resources. The growth of new models of computing, including cloud computing and publically available but privately held data repositories, opens up new possibilities for NSF. For example, by supporting some footprint in commercial cloud environments, many more NSF researchers could have the ability to access compute and data capabilities at a scale currently only available to a few researchers and commercial users. For some fields, this could be transformative.

One of the benefits of cloud computing is the flexible way in which resources are provided on demand to the users. Evidence from several studies suggests that this flexibility comes with a monetary cost (which may not be competitive with NSF-supported facilities) that must be balanced against the opportunity cost, in terms of scientific productivity, in the conventional model of allocations and jobs queues. On the other hand, virtualization, the implied ability to migrate work, and limited oversubscription can work to decrease overall costs, increase overall system throughput, and increase the ability of the system to meet fluctuating workloads, although perhaps at the expense of the performance of an individual job. The cost trade-offs are complicated and need to be looked at carefully.

The Role of Other Federal Agencies in Providing Advanced Computing

Researchers funded by one agency sometimes make use of computing resources provided by other federal agencies. Today, allocations are made by the agency that operates the advanced computing system on the basis of scientific merit and alignment with agency mission. Other arrangements are possible. NSF could directly purchase advanced computing services from another federal agency. It could also join with other agencies to contract from a commercial provider or coordinate with other agencies on specifying services and costs in developing requests for proposals for commercial services.

5. The committee seeks comments on the role that private industry and other federal agencies can play in providing advanced computing infrastructure—including the opportunities, costs, issues, and service models. It also seeks input on balancing the different costs and on making trade-offs in accessibly (e.g., guaranteeing on-demand access is more costly than providing best-effort access).

Allocation of Research Funding and Computing Resources

A particular issue that has surfaced in the committee's work so far is the "double jeopardy" that arises when researchers must clear two hurdles: getting their research proposals funded and getting their requests for computing resources allocated. Given the modest acceptance rates of both processes, such a process necessarily diminishes the chances that a researcher with a good idea can in fact carry out the proposed work. Relatedly, researchers also do not know in advance on what machine they will be granted an allocation, which may cause them to incur the cost and delay needed to "port" data and code to a new system (and possibly new system architecture) in order to use the allocation.

6. The committee seeks comments on the challenges facing researchers in obtaining allocations of computing resources and suggestions for improving the allocation and review processes for making advanced computing resources available to the research community.

3

Possible NSF Responses

BETTER UNDERSTANDING OF SCIENCE AND ENGINEERING OPPORTUNITIES, PRIORITIES, AND REQUIREMENTS FOR ADVANCED COMPUTING

Although the critical role of advanced computing in science and engineering is well understood and a number of reports have been prepared to address foundation-wide or disciplinary requirements, not all research areas or programs have defined their requirements for advanced computing or established processes for regularly updating and refining them, such as by constructing roadmaps that describe science and engineering goals and advanced computing resources needed. One example is the report of the Snowmass 2013 Computing Frontier Working Group on Lattice Field Theory.[1] Such analyses may provide additional useful information for understanding aggregate capability and capacity needs and expected trends in these needs, for understanding overall National Science Foundation (NSF) resource requirements, for prioritizing investments, and for aligning research program and supporting advanced computing investments. Such community-led efforts seem a natural fit for NSF.

---

[1] T. Blum, R.S. Van de Water, D. Holmgren, R. Brower, S. Catterall, N. Christ, A. Kronfeld, et al., Lattice field theory for the energy and intensity frontiers: Scientific goals and computing needs, Report of the Snowmass 2013 Computing Frontier working group on Lattice Field Theory, arXiv:1310.6087v1, submitted October 23, 2013.

7. *For its final report, the committee will explore and seeks comment on whether wider collection and more frequent updating of requirements for advanced computing could be used to inform strategic planning, priority setting, and resource allocation; how these requirements might be used; and how they might best be developed, collected, and aggregated.*

FUNCTIONAL RATHER THAN TECHNOLOGY-FOCUSED OR STRUCTURAL APPROACH TO UNDERSTANDING REQUIREMENTS AND ESTABLISHING PRIORITIES

In 2009, the NSF-wide Advisory Committee for Cyberinfrastructure (ACCI) established six task forces to investigate long-term cyberinfrastructure issues with a focus on its major elements, including high-performance computing, campus bridging, grand challenges, data, and software. Their final reports in 2011[2] provide detailed descriptions of the state of the major elements of NSF's advanced cyberinfrastructure ecosystem and recommendations for advancing them in support of research. New initiatives aligned with these recommendations have resulted in advances in the state of key elements of cyberinfrastructure, including software, data, hardware, and networking. At first glance, it is once again tempting to seek a structural approach similar to the one used in the ACCI task forces whereby one considers prioritizing investments for the major elements of the ecosystem, such as hardware, software, storage, etc. Such a structural approach could potentially lead to optimal solutions for each element by resolving the complex trade-offs that arise when these elements contend for resources.

However, none of these elements can be directly utilized by the science and engineering user community. In fact, scientists can effectively utilize infrastructure only when it is presented to them as an integrated whole encompassing appropriate hardware, software, data, networking, technical services, etc. Additionally, customizations to meet the requirements of workflows along broad thematic areas can further enhance utility to catalyze the next generation of scientific outcomes. In this approach, requirements can be used to understand the needed functional capabilities. The latter, in turn, could be used to inform how strategic investments should be made.

---

[2] See National Science Foundation, "ACCI—Task Forces," http://www.nsf.gov/cise/aci/taskforces (accessed September 25, 2014).

ENHANCED ORGANIZATIONAL STABILITY AND FLEXIBILITY OF NSF-FUNDED ADVANCED COMPUTING CENTERS

Any funding and organizational structure must balance organizational stability and sustainability against responsiveness to technological change and customer needs. NSF has long supported leading-edge cyberinfrastructure via a series of solicitations and open competitions. Although this has stimulated intellectual competition and increased NSF's financial leverage, it has also made deep and sustainable collaboration difficult among frequent competitors. Individual awardees, quite rationally, often focus more on maximizing their long-term probability of continued funding, rather than adapting and responding to community needs.

Frequent competitions can also make it more difficult for NSF-funded service providers to recruit and retain talented staff when the horizon for funding is only 2-5 years. This is especially true when the competition for information technology and computational science expertise with industry is so great. In contrast, longer horizons could also let NSF and its service providers evolve services and staffing in response to changing community needs and business partnerships. In turn, Major Research Equipment and Facilities Construction (MREFC) projects could coordinate and plan computing support and data analysis needs with NSF's cyberinfrastructure providers. Longer-term funding horizons could also allow service providers to work more collaboratively with NSF on responses to community needs, encourage inter-organizational collaboration, and facilitate longer-term budget planning and staged equipment acquisitions across multiple sites.

8. The committee seeks comments on the tension between the benefits of competition and the need for continuity as well as alternative models that might more clearly delineate the distinction between performance review and accountability and organizational continuity and service capabilities.

ENHANCED STRATEGIC PLANNING AND INTERNAL COORDINATION

Despite its vital role in science and engineering, the committee observes that advanced computing receives relatively little attention in the current NSF strategic plan, and decision making about advanced computing is distributed across the Division for Advanced Cyberinfrastructure, other divisions and division programs, the Major Research Instrumentation Program, and individual research institutions. Both coordination and strategic decision making seem especially important in an era of growing demand and cost, and place a premium on shared solutions where possible.

Top-down mandates often prove ineffective, even when the coordination is very much needed, and reaching consensus through "grass-roots" efforts may be too slow. Both top-down and bottom-up processes require mechanisms for identifying detailed needs of directorates and their programs and for ensuring adequate community input; the committee will be exploring and seeks comment on ways this might be done.

9. The committee seeks comments on how NSF might best coordinate and set overall strategy for advanced computing-related activities and investments as well as the relative merits of both formal, top-down coordination and enhanced, bottom-up process.

Appendixes

A

Biographies of Committee Members

WILLIAM GROPP, *Co-Chair,* is the Thomas M. Siebel Chair in Computer Science at the University of Illinois, Urbana-Champaign, where he is also founding director of the Parallel Computing Institute. He held the positions of assistant (1982-1988) and associate (1988-1990) professor in the Computer Science Department at Yale University. In 1990, he joined the Numerical Analysis Group at Argonne, where he was a senior computer scientist in the Mathematics and Computer Science Division, a senior scientist in the Department of Computer Science at the University of Chicago, and a senior fellow in the Argonne-Chicago Computation Institute. From 2000 through 2006, he was also deputy director of the Mathematics and Computer Science Division at Argonne. In 2007, he joined the University of Illinois, Urbana-Champaign, as the Paul and Cynthia Saylor Professor in the Department of Computer Science. In 2008, he was appointed deputy director for research for the Institute of Advanced Computing Applications and Technologies at the University of Illinois. His research interests are in parallel computing, software for scientific computing, and numerical methods for partial differential equations. He has played a major role in the development of the MPI message-passing standard, is one of the designers of the PETSc parallel numerical library, and has developed efficient and scalable parallel algorithms for the solution of linear and non-linear equations. Dr. Gropp is a fellow of the Association for Computing Machinery (ACM), the Institute of Electrical and Electronics Engineers (IEEE), and the Society for Industrial and Applied Mathematics (SIAM), and a member of the National Academy of Engineering. He received the Sidney Fernbach Award from the IEEE Computer Society in 2008 and the Technical Committee on Scalable Computing Award for Excellence in Scalable Computing in 2010. Dr. Gropp received his B.S. in mathematics from Case Western Reserve University, an M.S. in physics from the University of Washington, and a Ph.D. in computer science from Stanford University.

ROBERT HARRISON, *Co-Chair*, is the director, Institute of Advanced Scientific Computing, at Stony Brook University and director, Computational Science Center, Brookhaven National Laboratory. The core mission of the new Stony Brook institute is to advance the science of computing and its applications to solving complex problems in the physical sciences, the life sciences, medicine, sociology, industry, and finance. It works closely with the Brookhaven center, which specializes in data-intensive computing. Dr. Harrison's research interests are focused on scientific computing and the development of computational chemistry methods for the world's most technologically advanced supercomputers. From 2002 to 2012, he was director of the Joint Institute of Computational Science, professor of chemistry and corporate fellow at the University of Tennessee and Oak Ridge National Laboratory. Prior positions were at the Environmental Molecular Sciences Laboratory, Pacific Northwest Laboratory, and Argonne National Laboratory. He has a prolific career in high-performance computing with more than 100 publications on the subject, as well as extensive service on national advisory committees. He received his B.A. from Churchill College, University of Cambridge, and his Ph.D. in organic and theoretical chemistry from the University of Cambridge.

MARK ABBOTT is dean of the College of Earth, Ocean, and Atmospheric Sciences at Oregon State University (OSU). Dr. Abbott has been at OSU since 1988 and has been dean of the college since 2001. Prior to his appointments at OSU, he served as a member of the technical staff at the Jet Propulsion Laboratory (JPL) and as a research oceanographer at Scripps Institution of Oceanography. Dr. Abbott's research focuses on the interaction of biological and physical processes in the upper ocean and relies on both remote sensing and field observations. He is a pioneer in the use of satellite ocean color data to study coupled physical/biological processes. As part of a NASA Earth Observing System interdisciplinary science team, Dr. Abbott led an effort to link remotely sensed data of the Southern Ocean with coupled ocean circulation/ecosystem models. His field research included the first deployment of an array of bio-optical moorings in the Southern Ocean as part of the U.S. Joint Global Ocean Flux Study. Dr. Abbott was a member of the National Science Board from 2006 to 2012 and served as a consultant to the board until 2013. He is the vice chair of the Oregon Global Warming Commission. He is currently a member of the board of trustees for the Consortium for Ocean Leadership and the board of trustees of NEON, Inc. His past advisory posts include chairing the Coastal Ocean Applications and Science Team for NOAA and chairing the U.S. Joint Global Flux Study Science Steering Committee. He has also been a member of the Director's Advisory Council for the JPL and NASA's MODIS and SeaWiFS science teams and the Earth Observing System Investigators Working Group. He was the 2011 recipient of the Jim Gray eScience Award, presented by Microsoft Research. Dr. Abbott is a national associate member of the National Academies and is currently a member of the National Research Council's (NRC's) Space Studies Board, chair of the Committee on Earth Science and Applications from Space, a member of the Committee to Advise the U.S. Global Change Research Program, and a member of the Panel on the Review of the Draft 2013 National Climate Assessment (NCA) Report. Among his prolific NRC service, Dr. Abbott served on the NRC's Committee on Evaluating NASA's Strategic Direction, the Committee on the Assessment of NASA's Earth Science Programs, the Committee on the Role and Scope of Mission-Enabling Activities in NASA's Space and Earth Science Missions, and the Panel on Land-Use Change, Ecosystem Dynamics and Biodiversity for the 2007 Earth science and applications from space decadal survey. Dr. Abbott received his B.S. in conservation of natural resources from the University of California, Berkeley, and his Ph.D. in ecology from the University of California.

DAVID ARNETT is professor of astrophysics at the Steward Observatory of the University of Arizona. He is a theoretical astrophysicist who first demonstrated how explosive nucleosynthesis in supernovae produces the elements from carbon through iron and nickel. He constructed quantitative theoretical models of evolving massive stars and showed that the ejecta produce a good fit to the abundance of heavy elements in the galaxy. His research interests include nuclear astrophysics, formation of neutron stars and black holes, high-performance computers, theoretical physics, hydrodynamics, thermonuclear burning, stellar evolution, computer graphics, and computer modeling. Dr. Arnett is a member of the National Academy of Sciences. Dr. Arnett received his Ph.D. in physics from Yale University.

ROBERT GROSSMAN is a faculty member at the University of Chicago. He is the director of the Center for Data Intensive Science, a senior fellow and core faculty in the Computation Institute and the Institute for Genomics and Systems Biology, and a professor of medicine in the Section of Genetic Medicine. He also serves as the chief research informatics officer for the Biological Sciences Division. His research group focuses on data intensive computing, data science, and bioinformatics. He is the founder and a partner of Open Data Group, which provides analytic services to help companies build predictive models over big data, and is the director of the not-for-profit Open Cloud Consortium, which provides cloud computing infrastructure to support the research community. He was elected a fellow of the AAAS in 2013. Dr. Grossman earned his Ph.D. in applied mathematics at Princeton University and an A.B. in mathematics from Harvard University.

PETER KOGGE is a professor of computer science and engineering and concurrent professor of electrical engineering at the University of Notre Dame. Dr. Kogge was with IBM, Federal Systems Division, from 1968 until 1994, and was appointed an IEEE fellow in 1990, and an IBM fellow in 1993. In 1977 he was a visiting professor in the ECE Department at the University of Massachusetts, Amherst. From 1977 through 1994, he was also an adjunct professor in the Computer Science Department of the State University of New York at Binghamton. In 1994, he joined the University of Notre Dame as first holder of the endowed McCourtney Chair in Computer Science and Engineering (CSE). Starting in the summer of 1997, he has been a distinguished visiting scientist at the Center for Integrated Space Microsystems at JPL. He is also the research thrust leader for architecture in Notre Dame's Center for Nano Science and Technology. For the 2000-2001 academic year, he was the Interim Schubmehl-Prein Chairman of the CSE Department at Notre Dame. From August 2001 until December 2008, he was the associate dean for research, College of Engineering; since Fall 2003, he has been a concurrent professor of electrical engineering. His current research areas include massively parallel processing architectures, advanced VLSI and nano technologies and their relationship to computing systems architectures, non von Neumann models of programming and execution, parallel algorithms and applications, and their impact on computer architecture. While at IBM, one of his groups designed the first multi-processor PIM device with significant DRAM memory that may also, arguably, be the world's first multi-core chip. A paper on its architecture received the Daniel Slotnick Award at the 1994 International Conference on Parallel Processing. He also designed and built the RTAIS parallel processor. Prior parallel machines included the IBM 3838 Array Processor, and the space shuttle input/output processor (IOP), which probably represents the first true parallel processor to fly in space and is one of the earliest examples of multi-threaded architectures. Dr. Kogge received the IEEE Seymour Cray Award in 2012 and the IEEE Charles Babbage Award in 2014. He received his B.S. in electrical engineering from the University of Notre Dame, his M.S. in systems and engineering from Syracuse University, and his Ph.D. in electrical engineering from Stanford University.

PADMA RAGHAVAN is the associate vice president for research and director of strategic initiatives at the Pennsylvania State University, where she is also a distinguished professor of computer science and engineering. Dr. Raghavan is the founding director of the Penn State Institute for CyberScience, the coordinating unit on campus for developing interdisciplinary computation and data-enabled science and engineering. Prior to joining Penn State in 2000, she served as an associate professor in the Department of Computer Science at University of Tennessee. Her research is in the area of high-performance computing and computational science and engineering. She has more than 95 peer-reviewed publications in three major areas, including scalable parallel computing; energy-aware supercomputing, i.e., performance and power scalability of advanced computer systems; and computational modeling, simulation, and knowledge extraction. Dr. Raghavan currently serves on the editorial boards of the SIAM book series *Computational Science and Engineering* and *Software, Environments and Tools*, the *Journal of Parallel and Distributed Computing*, the *Journal of Computational Science*, and *IEEE Transactions on Parallel and Distributed Systems*. She serves on the program committees of major conferences sponsored by ACM, IEEE, and SIAM, and she co-chaired Technical Papers for Supercomputing 2012 and the 2011 SIAM Conference on Computational Science and Engineering. Dr. Raghavan also serves on various advisory and review boards, including the NRC Panel on Digitization and Communication Science, the Network for Earthquake Engineering Simulation, and the Computer Research Association's Committee on the Status of Women in Computing Research. She is a fellow of the IEEE, and she received an NSF CAREER Award and the Maria Goeppert-Mayer Distinguished Scholar Award from the University of Chicago and the Argonne National Laboratory for her research on parallel sparse matrix computations. Dr. Raghavan received her Ph.D. in computer science from Penn State.

DANIEL A. REED is currently vice president for research and economic development, as well as a professor of computer science, electrical and computer engineering, and medicine at the University of Iowa. He also holds the University Computational Science and Bioinformatics Chair at Iowa. Dr. Reed was a corporate vice president at Microsoft from 2009 to 2012, responsible for global technology policy and extreme computing, and director of scalable and multicore computing at Microsoft from 2007 until 2009. Prior to Microsoft, he was the founding director of the Renaissance Computing Institute at the University of North Carolina,

Chapel Hill, where he also served as Chancellor's Eminent Professor and vice chancellor for information technology. Before joining the University of North Carolina, Chapel Hill, in 2003, Dr. Reed was director of the National Center for Supercomputing Applications (NCSA), Gutgsell Professor and head of the Department of Computer Science at the University of Illinois, Urbana-Champaign. He was appointed to the President's Council of Advisors on Science and Technology (PCAST) by President Bush in 2006 and served on the President's Information Technology Advisory Committee (PITAC) from 2003-2005. As chair of PITAC's computational science subcommittee, he was lead author of the report *Computational Science: Ensuring America's Competitiveness*. On PCAST, he co-chaired the Networking and Information Technology subcommittee (with George Scalise of the Semiconductor Industry Association) and co-authored a report on the Networking and Information Technology Research and Development (NITRD) program called *Leadership Under Challenge: Information Technology R&D in Competitive World*. Dr. Reed is the past chair of the board of directors of the Computing Research Association (CRA) and currently serves on its Government Affairs Committee. CRA represents the research interests of the university, national laboratory, and industrial research laboratory communities in computing across North America. He received his B.S. from the University of Missouri, Rolla, and his M.S. and Ph.D. degrees from Purdue University, all in computer science.

VALERIE TAYLOR is the senior associate dean of academic affairs in the Dwight Look College of Engineering and the regents professor and Royce E. Wisenbaker Professor in the Department of Computer Science and Engineering at Texas A&M University. In 2003, she joined Texas A&M as the department head of Computer Science and Engineering, where she remained in that position until 2011. Prior to joining Texas A&M, Dr. Taylor was a member of the faculty in the Electrical Engineering and Computer Sciences Department at Northwestern University for 11 years. She has authored or coauthored more than 100 papers in the area of high-performance computing. She is also the executive director of the Center for Minorities and People with Disabilities in IT. Dr. Taylor is an IEEE fellow and has received numerous awards for distinguished research and leadership, including the 2001 IEEE Harriet B. Rigas Award for a woman with significant contributions in engineering education, the 2002 Outstanding Young Engineering Alumni from the University of California, Berkeley, the 2002 CRA Nico Habermann Award for increasing the diversity in computing, and the 2005 Tapia Achievement Award for Scientific Scholarship, Civic Science, and Diversifying Computing. Dr. Taylor is a member of the ACM. She earned her B.S. in electrical and computer engineering and M.S. in computer engineering from Purdue

University and a Ph.D. in electrical engineering and computer sciences from the University of California, Berkeley.

KATHERINE YELICK is a professor of electrical engineering and computer sciences at the University of California, Berkeley, and the associate laboratory director for computing sciences at Lawrence Berkeley National Laboratory. Dr. Yelick is known for her research in parallel languages, compilers, algorithms, and libraries. She co-invented the UPC and Titanium languages and developed analyses, optimizations, and runtime systems for their implementation. She has also done research on memory hierarchy optimizations, communication-avoiding algorithms, and automatic performance tuning, including developing the first autotuned sparse matrix library. In her current role as associate laboratory director, she manages an organization that includes National Energy Research Scientific Computing Center (NERSC), the Energy Science Network (ESNet), and the Computational Research Division. She was the director of NERSC from 2008 to 2012. Dr. Yelick has received multiple research and teaching awards, including the Athena award, and she is an ACM fellow and an IEEE senior member. She is a member of the California Council on Science and Technology, the NRC Computer Science and Telecommunications Board (CSTB), and the Science and Technology Committee overseeing research at Los Alamos and Lawrence Livermore National Laboratories. She earned her Ph.D. in electrical engineering and computer science from the Massachusetts Institute of Technology.

B

Questions on Directions and Needs for Advanced Cyberinfrastructure

The committee seeks input from the community on the directions and needs for cyber infrastructure and provides a list of key issues in the body of the report. This appendix contains additional issues and questions on which the committee will be asking input. *The committee seeks both responses to these questions and suggestions for other issues on which to request input.*

GENERAL ISSUES

- The trajectory and relevance of large-scale simulation's impact on foundational advances in science and engineering.
- Scientific research grand challenges that will be substantially advanced by large-scale data analytics and data mining not currently possible in research infrastructures.
- Areas for research about cyberinfrastructure investments (e.g., emergent technologies and algorithms, balance between experimental and "production" systems, education and workforce development, community software) required to support sustained advances in U.S. science.
- Challenges and responses by research infrastructures at all scales (e.g., campus, regional, national; problem-focused or multipurpose) to the items above, identifying those that can be most positively affected by the National Science Foundation (NSF). These should encompass economic, cross-agency, and international considerations.

APPENDIX B

QUESTIONS FOR USERS OF ADVANCED COMPUTING INFRASTRUCTURE

1. *Research needs/opportunities*
   a. What are some of the open problems in your field that require large-scale simulation to solve? Which might lead to fundamental or foundational advances? Why are these problems not being solved today?
   b. What are some of the open problems in your field that require data-intensive computing, such as large-scale data analytics and data mining? Why are these problems not being solved today?
   c. Are there plans or roadmaps that characterize future computing needs in your field?
   d. What types of new workflows are emerging that require complex access pathways between data sets, computation, and storage?
2. *Advanced computing capabilities, facilities, requirements*
   e. What forms of computing are used in your field? For example, How does your field make use of laptop/desktops, research group clusters, department or campus commodity cluster systems, mid- to large-scale, shared capacity systems such as XSEDE, leadership-class capability systems such as Blue Waters (NSF) or Mira (Department of Energy), or commercial cloud services such as Amazon EC2? How would you characterize the importance of access to each type—required, desirable, or unnecessary? How might these needs change in the future, and why?
   f. How are data sets evolving in terms of variety and distribution? Do you access tens to hundreds of near-real-time data sets? Do you rely on a few large repositories?
   g. With computer hardware and software evolving more rapidly than in the recent past, what impacts do you see for your field? For example, what role will new hardware such as accelerators (GPUs or Intel Xeon Phi), FPGAs, new memory systems, or new I/O systems play? Are there barriers to their adoption, such as challenges making necessary modifications to software?
   h. What software does your field depend on? Who develops and maintains this code, and how is this work supported?
   i. Is your field keeping up the technical skills needed to use new technical capabilities?
3. *Challenges and suggestions*
   j. What are the biggest challenges that your field faces in using computation? Consider access to systems with sufficient capability and capacity; productivity of environments; algorithms; workforce; stability of software and hardware; and the ability to use systems efficiently, including parallelism and scalability.

k. What investments would have the greatest positive impact on your research field? For example, this could be more computer systems to increase access, different kinds of systems with a different balance of capability, support for community software, development of new algorithms, or a workforce with better training in computational science.
l. What other elements of national cyber infrastructure would significantly advance the pace of discovery or expand participation? Examples might include shared file systems or standard services and application program interfaces.